# Amours De Voyage

Arthur Hugh Clough

## Alpha Editions

This Edition Published in 2021

ISBN: 9789355119995

Design and Setting By
**Alpha Editions**
www.alphaedis.com
Email – info@alphaedis.com

# TABLE OF CONTENTS

# Canto I

*Over the great windy waters, and over the clear-crested summits,*
  *Unto the sun and the sky, and unto the perfecter earth,*
*Come, let us go,—to a land wherein gods of the old time wandered,*
  *Where every breath even now changes to ether divine.*
*Come, let us go; though withal a voice whisper, 'The world that we live in,*
  *Whithersoever we turn, still is the same narrow crib;*
*'Tis but to prove limitation, and measure a cord, that we travel;*
  *Let who would 'scape and be free go to his chamber and think;*
*'Tis but to change idle fancies for memories wilfully falser;*
  *'Tis but to go and have been.'—Come, little bark! let us go.*
*I. Claude to Eustace.*


*Dear Eustatio, I write that you may write me an answer,*
*Or at the least to put us again en rapport with each other.*
*Rome disappoints me much,—St Peter's, perhaps, in especial;*
*Only the Arch of Titus and view from the Lateran please me:*
*This, however, perhaps is the weather, which truly is horrid.*
*Greece must be better, surely; and yet I am feeling so spiteful,*
*That I could travel to Athens, to Delphi, and Troy, and Mount Sinai,*
*Though but to see with my eyes that these are vanity also.*
  *Rome disappoints me much; I hardly as yet understand it, but*
*RUBBISHY seems the word that most exactly would suit it.*
*All the foolish destructions, and all the sillier savings,*
*All the incongruous things of past incompatible ages,*
*Seem to be treasured up here to make fools of present and future.*
*Would to Heaven the old Goths had made a cleaner sweep of it!*

*Would to Heaven some new ones would come and destroy these churches!*

*However, one can live in Rome as also in London.*

*It is a blessing, no doubt, to be rid, at least for a time, of*

*All one's friends and relations,—yourself (forgive me!) included,—*

*All the assujettissement of having been what one has been,*

*What one thinks one is, or thinks that others suppose one;*

*Yet, in despite of all, we turn like fools to the English.*

*Vernon has been my fate; who is here the same that you knew him,—*

*Making the tour, it seems, with friends of the name of Trevellyn.*

*II. Claude to Eustace.*


*Rome disappoints me still; but I shrink and adapt myself to it.*

*Somehow a tyrannous sense of a superincumbent oppression*

*Still, wherever I go, accompanies ever, and makes me*

*Feel like a tree (shall I say?) buried under a ruin of brickwork.*

*Rome, believe me, my friend, is like its own Monte Testaceo,*

*Merely a marvellous mass of broken and castaway wine-pots.*

*Ye gods! what do I want with this rubbish of ages departed,*

*Things that Nature abhors, the experiments that she has failed in?*

*What do I find in the Forum? An archway and two or three pillars.*

*Well, but St. Peter's? Alas, Bernini has filled it with sculpture!*

*No one can cavil, I grant, at the size of the great Coliseum.*

*Doubtless the notion of grand and capacious and massive amusement,*

*This the old Romans had; but tell me, is this an idea?*

*Yet of solidity much, but of splendour little is extant:*

*'Brickwork I found thee, and marble I left thee!' their Emperor vaunted;*

*'Marble I thought thee, and brickwork I find thee!' the Tourist may answer.*

*III. Georgina Trevellyn to Louisa ——.*

*At last, dearest Louisa, I take up my pen to address you.*

*Here we are, you see, with the seven-and-seventy boxes,*

*Courier, Papa and Mamma, the children, and Mary and Susan:*

*Here we all are at Rome, and delighted of course with St. Peter's,*

*And very pleasantly lodged in the famous Piazza di Spagna.*

*Rome is a wonderful place, but Mary shall tell you about it;*

*Not very gay, however; the English are mostly at Naples;*

*There are the A.'s, we hear, and most of the W. party.*

*George, however, is come; did I tell you about his mustachios?*

*Dear, I must really stop, for the carriage, they tell me, is waiting;*

*Mary will finish; and Susan is writing, they say, to Sophia.*

*Adieu, dearest Louise,—evermore your faithful Georgina.*

*Who can a Mr. Claude be whom George has taken to be with?*

*Very stupid, I think, but George says so VERY clever.*

*IV. Claude to Eustace.*


*No, the Christian faith, as at any rate I understood it,*

*With its humiliations and exaltations combining,*

*Exaltations sublime, and yet diviner abasements,*

*Aspirations from something most shameful here upon earth and*

*In our poor selves to something most perfect above in the heavens,—*

*No, the Christian faith, as I, at least, understood it,*

*Is not here, O Rome, in any of these thy churches;*

*Is not here, but in Freiburg, or Rheims, or Westminster Abbey.*

*What in thy Dome I find, in all thy recenter efforts,*

*Is a something, I think, more RATIONAL far, more earthly,*

*Actual, less ideal, devout not in scorn and refusal,*

*But in a positive, calm, Stoic-Epicurean acceptance.*

*This I begin to detect in St. Peter's and some of the churches,*

*Mostly in all that I see of the sixteenth-century masters;*
*Overlaid of course with infinite gauds and gewgaws,*
*Innocent, playful follies, the toys and trinkets of childhood,*
*Forced on maturer years, as the serious one thing needful,*
*By the barbarian will of the rigid and ignorant Spaniard.*
　*Curious work, meantime, re-entering society: how we*
*Walk a livelong day, great Heaven, and watch our shadows!*
*What our shadows seem, forsooth, we will ourselves be.*
*Do I look like that? you think me that: then I AM that.*
*V. Claude to Eustace.*


*Luther, they say, was unwise; like a half-taught German, he could not*
*See that old follies were passing most tranquilly out of remembrance;*
*Leo the Tenth was employing all efforts to clear out abuses;*
*Jupiter, Juno, and Venus, Fine Arts, and Fine Letters, the Poets,*
*Scholars, and Sculptors, and Painters, were quietly clearing away the*
*Martyrs, and Virgins, and Saints, or at any rate Thomas Aquinas:*
*He must forsooth make a fuss and distend his huge Wittenberg lungs, and*
*Bring back Theology once yet again in a flood upon Europe:*
*Lo you, for forty days from the windows of heaven it fell; the*
*Waters prevail on the earth yet more for a hundred and fifty;*
*Are they abating at last? the doves that are sent to explore are*
*Wearily fain to return, at the best with a leaflet of promise,—*
*Fain to return, as they went, to the wandering wave-tost vessel,—*
*Fain to re-enter the roof which covers the clean and the unclean,—*
*Luther, they say, was unwise; he didn't see how things were going;*
*Luther was foolish,—but, O great God! what call you Ignatius?*
*O my tolerant soul, be still! but you talk of barbarians,*
*Alaric, Attila, Genseric;—why, they came, they killed, they*

Ravaged, and went on their way; but these vile, tyrannous Spaniards,
These are here still,—how long, O ye heavens, in the country of Dante?
These, that fanaticized Europe, which now can forget them, release not
This, their choicest of prey, this Italy; here you see them,—
Here, with emasculate pupils and gimcrack churches of Gesu,
Pseudo-learning and lies, confessional-boxes and postures,—
Here, with metallic beliefs and regimental devotions,—
Here, overcrusting with slime, perverting, defacing, debasing,
Michael Angelo's Dome, that had hung the Pantheon in heaven,
Raphael's Joys and Graces, and thy clear stars, Galileo!
VI. Claude to Eustace.


Which of three Misses Trevellyn it is that Vernon shall marry
Is not a thing to be known; for our friend is one of those natures
Which have their perfect delight in the general tender-domestic,
So that he trifles with Mary's shawl, ties Susan's bonnet,
Dances with all, but at home is most, they say, with Georgina,
Who is, however, TOO silly in my apprehension for Vernon.
I, as before when I wrote, continue to see them a little;
Not that I like them much or care a bajocco for Vernon,
But I am slow at Italian, have not many English acquaintance,
And I am asked, in short, and am not good at excuses.
Middle-class people these, bankers very likely, not wholly
Pure of the taint of the shop; will at table d'hote and restaurant
Have their shilling's worth, their penny's pennyworth even:
Neither man's aristocracy this, nor God's, God knoweth!
Yet they are fairly descended, they give you to know, well connected;
Doubtless somewhere in some neighbourhood have, and are careful to keep, some
Threadbare-genteel relations, who in their turn are enchanted

*Grandly among county people to introduce at assemblies*

*To the unpennied cadets our cousins with excellent fortunes.*

*Neither man's aristocracy this, nor God's, God knoweth!*

*VII. Claude to Eustace.*


*Ah, what a shame, indeed, to abuse these most worthy people!*

*Ah, what a sin to have sneered at their innocent rustic pretensions!*

*Is it not laudable really, this reverent worship of station?*

*Is it not fitting that wealth should tender this homage to culture?*

*Is it not touching to witness these efforts, if little availing,*

*Painfully made, to perform the old ritual service of manners?*

*Shall not devotion atone for the absence of knowledge? and fervour*

*Palliate, cover, the fault of a superstitious observance?*

*Dear, dear, what do I say? but, alas! just now, like Iago,*

*I can be nothing at all, if it is not critical wholly;*

*So in fantastic height, in coxcomb exaltation,*

*Here in the garden I walk, can freely concede to the Maker*

*That the works of His hand are all very good: His creatures,*

*Beast of the field and fowl, He brings them before me; I name them;*

*That which I name them, they are,—the bird, the beast, and the cattle.*

*But for Adam,—alas, poor critical coxcomb Adam!*

*But for Adam there is not found an help-meet for him.*

*VIII. Claude to Eustace.*


*No, great Dome of Agrippa, thou art not Christian! canst not,*

*Strip and replaster and daub and do what they will with thee, be so!*

*Here underneath the great porch of colossal Corinthian columns,*

*Here as I walk, do I dream of the Christian belfries above them?*

*Or, on a bench as I sit and abide for long hours, till thy whole vast*

*Round grows dim as in dreams to my eyes, I repeople thy niches,*
*Not with the Martyrs, and Saints, and Confessors, and Virgins, and children,*
*But with the mightier forms of an older, austerer worship;*
*And I recite to myself, how*

       *Eager for battle here*
     *Stood Vulcan, here matronal Juno,*
      *And with the bow to his shoulder faithful*
     *He who with pure dew laveth of Castaly*
     *His flowing locks, who holdeth of Lycia*
     *The oak forest and the wood that bore him,*
      *Delos' and Patara's own Apollo. [*]*


   *      Hic avidus stetit*
    *Vulcanus, hic matrona Juno, et*
     *Nunquam humeris positurus arcum;*
   *Qui rore puro Castaliae lavit*
   *Crines solutos, qui Lyciae tenet*
    *Dumeta natalemque silvam,*
     *Delius et Patareus Apollo.*

*IX. Claude to Eustace.*


*Yet it is pleasant, I own it, to be in their company; pleasant,*
*Whatever else it may be, to abide in the feminine presence.*
*Pleasant, but wrong, will you say? But this happy, serene coexistence*
*Is to some poor soft souls, I fear, a necessity simple,*
*Meat and drink and life, and music, filling with sweetness,*
*Thrilling with melody sweet, with harmonies strange overwhelming,*
*All the long-silent strings of an awkward, meaningless fabric.*
*Yet as for that, I could live, I believe, with children; to have those*

*Pure and delicate forms encompassing, moving about you,*
*This were enough, I could think; and truly with glad resignation*
*Could from the dream of Romance, from the fever of flushed adolescence,*
*Look to escape and subside into peaceful avuncular functions.*
*Nephews and nieces! alas, for as yet I have none! and, moreover,*
*Mothers are jealous, I fear me, too often, too rightfully; fathers*
*Think they have title exclusive to spoiling their own little darlings;*
*And by the law of the land, in despite of Malthusian doctrine,*
*No sort of proper provision is made for that most patriotic,*
*Most meritorious subject, the childless and bachelor uncle.*
*X. Claude to Eustace.*


*Ye, too, marvellous Twain, that erect on the Monte Cavallo*
*Stand by your rearing steeds in the grace of your motionless movement,*
*Stand with your upstretched arms and tranquil regardant faces,*
*Stand as instinct with life in the might of immutable manhood,—*
*O ye mighty and strange, ye ancient divine ones of Hellas.*
*Are ye Christian too? to convert and redeem and renew you,*
*Will the brief form have sufficed, that a Pope has set up on the apex*
*Of the Egyptian stone that o'ertops you, the Christian symbol?*
  *And ye, silent, supreme in serene and victorious marble,*
*Ye that encircle the walls of the stately Vatican chambers,*
*Juno and Ceres, Minerva, Apollo, the Muses and Bacchus,*
*Ye unto whom far and near come posting the Christian pilgrims,*
*Ye that are ranged in the halls of the mystic Christian Pontiff,*
*Are ye also baptized? are ye of the kingdom of Heaven?*
*Utter, O some one, the word that shall reconcile Ancient and Modern!*
*Am I to turn me from this unto thee, great Chapel of Sixtus?*
*XI. Claude to Eustace.*

*These are the facts. The uncle, the elder brother, the squire (a*

*Little embarrassed, I fancy), resides in the family place in*

*Cornwall, of course; 'Papa is in business,' Mary informs me;*

*He's a good sensible man, whatever his trade is. The mother*

*Is—shall I call it fine?—herself she would tell you refined, and*

*Greatly, I fear me, looks down on my bookish and maladroit manners;*

*Somewhat affecteth the blue; would talk to me often of poets;*

*Quotes, which I hate, Childe Harold; but also appreciates Wordsworth;*

*Sometimes adventures on Schiller; and then to religion diverges;*

*Questions me much about Oxford; and yet, in her loftiest flights still*

*Grates the fastidious ear with the slightly mercantile accent.*


*Is it contemptible, Eustace—I'm perfectly ready to think so,—*

*Is it,—the horrible pleasure of pleasing inferior people?*

*I am ashamed of my own self; and yet true it is, if disgraceful,*

*That for the first time in life I am living and moving with freedom.*

*I, who never could talk to the people I meet with my uncle,—*

*I, who have always failed,—I, trust me, can suit the Trevellyns;*

*I, believe me,—great conquest, am liked by the country bankers.*

*And I am glad to be liked, and like in return very kindly.*

*So it proceeds; laissez faire, laissez aller,—such is the watchword.*

*Well, I know there are thousands as pretty and hundreds as pleasant,*

*Girls by the dozen as good, and girls in abundance with polish*

*Higher and manners more perfect than Susan or Mary Trevellyn.*

*Well, I know, after all, it is only juxtaposition,—*

*Juxtaposition, in short; and what is juxtaposition?*

*XII. Claude to Eustace.*

*But I am in for it now,—laissez faire, of a truth, laissez aller.*

*Yes, I am going,—I feel it, I feel and cannot recall it,—*

*Fusing with this thing and that, entering into all sorts of relations,*

*Tying I know not what ties, which, whatever they are, I know one thing,*

*Will, and must, woe is me, be one day painfully broken,—*

*Broken with painful remorses, with shrinkings of soul, and relentings,*

*Foolish delays, more foolish evasions, most foolish renewals.*

*But I have made the step, have quitted the ship of Ulysses;*

*Quitted the sea and the shore, passed into the magical island;*

*Yet on my lips is the moly, medicinal, offered of Hermes.*

*I have come into the precinct, the labyrinth closes around me,*

*Path into path rounding slyly; I pace slowly on, and the fancy,*

*Struggling awhile to sustain the long sequences, weary, bewildered,*

*Fain must collapse in despair; I yield, I am lost, and know nothing;*

*Yet in my bosom unbroken remaineth the clue; I shall use it.*

*Lo, with the rope on my loins I descend through the fissure; I sink, yet*

*Inly secure in the strength of invisible arms up above me;*

*Still, wheresoever I swing, wherever to shore, or to shelf, or*

*Floor of cavern untrodden, shell sprinkled, enchanting, I know I*

*Yet shall one time feel the strong cord tighten about me,—*

*Feel it, relentless, upbear me from spots I would rest in; and though the*

*Rope sway wildly, I faint, crags wound me, from crag unto crag re-*

*Bounding, or, wide in the void, I die ten deaths, ere the end I*

*Yet shall plant firm foot on the broad lofty spaces I quit, shall*

*Feel underneath me again the great massy strengths of abstraction,*

*Look yet abroad from the height o'er the sea whose salt wave I have tasted.*

*XIII. Georgina Trevellyn to Louisa ———.*

*Dearest Louisa,—Inquire, if you please, about Mr. Claude ———.*

*He has been once at R., and remembers meeting the H.'s.*
*Harriet L., perhaps, may be able to tell you about him.*
*It is an awkward youth, but still with very good manners;*
*Not without prospects, we hear; and, George says, highly connected.*
*Georgy declares it absurd, but Mamma is alarmed, and insists he has*
*Taken up strange opinions, and may be turning a Papist.*
*Certainly once he spoke of a daily service he went to.*
*'Where?' we asked, and he laughed and answered, 'At the Pantheon.'*
*This was a temple, you know, and now is a Catholic church; and*
*Though it is said that Mazzini has sold it for Protestant service,*
*Yet I suppose this change can hardly as yet be effected.*
*Adieu again,—evermore, my dearest, your loving Georgina.*

*P.S. by Mary Trevellyn.*

*I am to tell you, you say, what I think of our last new acquaintance.*
*Well, then, I think that George has a very fair right to be jealous.*
*I do not like him much, though I do not dislike being with him.*
*He is what people call, I suppose, a superior man, and*
*Certainly seems so to me; but I think he is terribly selfish.*

---

*Alba, thou findest me still, and, Alba, thou findest me ever,*
*Now from the Capitol steps, now over Titus's Arch,*
*Here from the large grassy spaces that spread from the Lateran portal,*
*Towering o'er aqueduct lines lost in perspective between,*
*Or from a Vatican window, or bridge, or the high Coliseum,*
*Clear by the garlanded line cut of the Flavian ring.*
*Beautiful can I not call thee, and yet thou hast power to o'ermaster,*

*Power of mere beauty; in dreams, Alba, thou hauntest me still.*
*Is it religion? I ask me; or is it a vain superstition?*
*Slavery abject and gross? service, too feeble, of truth?*
*Is it an idol I bow to, or is it a god that I worship?*
*Do I sink back on the old, or do I soar from the mean?*
*So through the city I wander and question, unsatisfied ever,*
*Reverent so I accept, doubtful because I revere.*

# Canto II

*Is it illusion? or does there a spirit from perfecter ages,*

    *Here, even yet, amid loss, change, and corruption abide?*

*Does there a spirit we know not, though seek, though we find, comprehend not,*

    *Here to entice and confuse, tempt and evade us, abide?*

*Lives in the exquisite grace of the column disjointed and single,*

    *Haunts the rude masses of brick garlanded gaily with vine,*

*E'en in the turret fantastic surviving that springs from the ruin,*

    *E'en in the people itself? is it illusion or not?*

*Is it illusion or not that attracteth the pilgrim transalpine,*

    *Brings him a dullard and dunce hither to pry and to stare?*

*Is it illusion or not that allures the barbarian stranger,*

    *Brings him with gold to the shrine, brings him in arms to the gate?*

*I. Claude to Eustace.*


*What do the people say, and what does the government do?—you*

*Ask, and I know not at all.  Yet fortune will favour your hopes; and*

*I, who avoided it all, am fated, it seems, to describe it.*

*I, who nor meddle nor make in politics,—I who sincerely*

*Put not my trust in leagues nor any suffrage by ballot,*

*Never predicted Parisian millenniums, never beheld a*

*New Jerusalem coming down dressed like a bride out of heaven*

*Right on the Place de la Concorde,—I, nevertheless, let me say it,*

*Could in my soul of souls, this day, with the Gaul at the gates shed*

*One true tear for thee, thou poor little Roman Republic;*

*What, with the German restored, with Sicily safe to the Bourbon,*

*Not leave one poor corner for native Italian exertion?*

*France, it is foully done! and you, poor foolish England,—*
*You, who a twelvemonth ago said nations must choose for themselves, you*
*Could not, of course, interfere,—you, now, when a nation has chosen——*
*Pardon this folly! The Times will, of course, have announced the occasion,*
*Told you the news of to-day; and although it was slightly in error*
*When it proclaimed as a fact the Apollo was sold to a Yankee,*
*You may believe when it tells you the French are at Civita Vecchia.*
*II. Claude to Eustace.*


*Dulce it is, and decorum, no doubt, for the country to fall,—to*
*Offer one's blood an oblation to Freedom, and die for the Cause; yet*
*Still, individual culture is also something, and no man*
*Finds quite distinct the assurance that he of all others is called on,*
*Or would be justified even, in taking away from the world that*
*Precious creature, himself. Nature sent him here to abide here;*
*Else why send him at all? Nature wants him still, it is likely;*
*On the whole, we are meant to look after ourselves; it is certain*
*Each has to eat for himself, digest for himself, and in general*
*Care for his own dear life, and see to his own preservation;*
*Nature's intentions, in most things uncertain, in this are decisive;*
*Which, on the whole, I conjecture the Romans will follow, and I shall.*
  *So we cling to our rocks like limpets; Ocean may bluster,*
*Over and under and round us; we open our shells to imbibe our*
*Nourishment, close them again, and are safe, fulfilling the purpose*
*Nature intended,—a wise one, of course, and a noble, we doubt not.*
*Sweet it may be and decorous, perhaps, for the country to die; but,*
*On the whole, we conclude the Romans won't do it, and I sha'n't.*
*III. Claude to Eustace.*

*Will they fight? They say so. And will the French? I can hardly,*
*Hardly think so; and yet——He is come, they say, to Palo,*
*He is passed from Monterone, at Santa Severa*
*He hath laid up his guns. But the Virgin, the Daughter of Roma,*
*She hath despised thee and laughed thee to scorn,—The Daughter of Tiber,*
*She hath shaken her head and built barricades against thee!*
*Will they fight? I believe it. Alas! 'tis ephemeral folly,*
*Vain and ephemeral folly, of course, compared with pictures,*
*Statues, and antique gems!—Indeed: and yet indeed too,*
*Yet, methought, in broad day did I dream,—tell it not in St. James's,*
*Whisper it not in thy courts, O Christ Church!—yet did I, waking,*
*Dream of a cadence that sings, Si tombent nos jeunes heros, la*
*Terre en produit de nouveaux contre vous tous prets a se battre;*
*Dreamt of great indignations and angers transcendental,*
*Dreamt of a sword at my side and a battle-horse underneath me.*
*IV. Claude to Eustace.*


*Now supposing the French or the Neapolitan soldier*
*Should by some evil chance come exploring the Maison Serny*
*(Where the family English are all to assemble for safety),*
*Am I prepared to lay down my life for the British female?*
*Really, who knows? One has bowed and talked, till, little by little,*
*All the natural heat has escaped of the chivalrous spirit.*
*Oh, one conformed, of course; but one doesn't die for good manners,*
*Stab or shoot, or be shot, by way of graceful attention.*
*No, if it should be at all, it should be on the barricades there;*
*Should I incarnadine ever this inky pacifical finger,*
*Sooner far should it be for this vapour of Italy's freedom,*
*Sooner far by the side of the d——d and dirty plebeians.*

*Ah, for a child in the street I could strike; for the full-blown lady——*

*Somehow, Eustace, alas! I have not felt the vocation.*

*Yet these people of course will expect, as of course, my protection,*

*Vernon in radiant arms stand forth for the lovely Georgina,*

*And to appear, I suppose, were but common civility.  Yes, and*

*Truly I do not desire they should either be killed or offended.*

*Oh, and of course, you will say, 'When the time comes, you will be ready.'*

*Ah, but before it comes, am I to presume it will be so?*

*What I cannot feel now, am I to suppose that I shall feel?*

*Am I not free to attend for the ripe and indubious instinct?*

*Am I forbidden to wait for the clear and lawful perception?*

*Is it the calling of man to surrender his knowledge and insight,*

*For the mere venture of what may, perhaps, be the virtuous action?*

*Must we, walking our earth, discerning a little, and hoping*

*Some plain visible task shall yet for our hands be assigned us,—*

*Must we abandon the future for fear of omitting the present,*

*Quit our own fireside hopes at the alien call of a neighbour,*

*To the mere possible shadow of Deity offer the victim?*

*And is all this, my friend, but a weak and ignoble refining,*

*Wholly unworthy the head or the heart of Your Own Correspondent?*

*V. Claude to Eustace.*


*Yes, we are fighting at last, it appears.  This morning as usual,*

*Murray, as usual, in hand, I enter the Caffe Nuovo;*

*Seating myself with a sense as it were of a change in the weather,*

*Not understanding, however, but thinking mostly of Murray,*

*And, for to-day is their day, of the Campidoglio Marbles;*

*Caffe-latte! I call to the waiter,—and Non c'e latte,*

*This is the answer he makes me, and this is the sign of a battle.*

*So I sit: and truly they seem to think any one else more*
*Worthy than me of attention.  I wait for my milkless nero,*
*Free to observe undistracted all sorts and sizes of persons,*
*Blending civilian and soldier in strangest costume, coming in, and*
*Gulping in hottest haste, still standing, their coffee,—withdrawing*
*Eagerly, jangling a sword on the steps, or jogging a musket*
*Slung to the shoulder behind.  They are fewer, moreover, than usual,*
*Much and silenter far; and so I begin to imagine*
*Something is really afloat.  Ere I leave, the Caffe is empty,*
*Empty too the streets, in all its length the Corso*
*Empty, and empty I see to my right and left the Condotti.*

*  Twelve o'clock, on the Pincian Hill, with lots of English,*
*Germans, Americans, French,—the Frenchmen, too, are protected,—*
*So we stand in the sun, but afraid of a probable shower;*
*So we stand and stare, and see, to the left of St. Peter's,*
*Smoke, from the cannon, white,—but that is at intervals only,—*
*Black, from a burning house, we suppose, by the Cavalleggieri;*
*And we believe we discern some lines of men descending*
*Down through the vineyard-slopes, and catch a bayonet gleaming.*
*Every ten minutes, however,—in this there is no misconception,—*
*Comes a great white puff from behind Michel Angelo's dome, and*
*After a space the report of a real big gun,—not the Frenchman's!—*
*That must be doing some work.  And so we watch and conjecture.*

*  Shortly, an Englishman comes, who says he has been to St. Peter's,*
*Seen the Piazza and troops, but that is all he can tell us;*
*So we watch and sit, and, indeed, it begins to be tiresome.—*
*All this smoke is outside; when it has come to the inside,*
*It will be time, perhaps, to descend and retreat to our houses.*

*  Half-past one, or two.  The report of small arms frequent,*

*Sharp and savage indeed; that cannot all be for nothing:*
*So we watch and wonder; but guessing is tiresome, very.*
*Weary of wondering, watching, and guessing, and gossiping idly,*
*Down I go, and pass through the quiet streets with the knots of*
*National Guards patrolling, and flags hanging out at the windows,*
*English, American, Danish,—and, after offering to help an*
*Irish family moving en masse to the Maison Serny,*
*After endeavouring idly to minister balm to the trembling*
*Quinquagenarian fears of two lone British spinsters,*
*Go to make sure of my dinner before the enemy enter.*
*But by this there are signs of stragglers returning; and voices*
*Talk, though you don't believe it, of guns and prisoners taken;*
*And on the walls you read the first bulletin of the morning.—*
*This is all that I saw, and all that I know of the battle.*
*VI. Claude to Eustace.*


*Victory! Victory!—Yes! ah, yes, thou republican Zion,*
*Truly the kings of the earth are gathered and gone by together;*
*Doubtless they marvelled to witness such things, were astonished, and so forth.*
*Victory! Victory! Victory!—Ah, but it is, believe me,*
*Easier, easier far, to intone the chant of the martyr*
*Than to indite any paean of any victory.  Death may*
*Sometimes be noble; but life, at the best, will appear an illusion.*
*While the great pain is upon us, it is great; when it is over,*
*Why, it is over.  The smoke of the sacrifice rises to heaven,*
*Of a sweet savour, no doubt, to Somebody; but on the altar,*
*Lo, there is nothing remaining but ashes and dirt and ill odour.*
  *So it stands, you perceive; the labial muscles that swelled with*
*Vehement evolution of yesterday Marseillaises,*

*Articulations sublime of defiance and scorning, to-day col-*

*Lapse and languidly mumble, while men and women and papers*

*Scream and re-scream to each other the chorus of Victory. Well, but*

*I am thankful they fought, and glad that the Frenchmen were beaten.*

*VII. Claude to Eustace.*


*So, I have seen a man killed! An experience that, among others!*

*Yes, I suppose I have; although I can hardly be certain,*

*And in a court of justice could never declare I had seen it.*

*But a man was killed, I am told, in a place where I saw*

*Something; a man was killed, I am told, and I saw something.*

  *I was returning home from St. Peter's; Murray, as usual,*

*Under my arm, I remember; had crossed the St. Angelo bridge; and*

*Moving towards the Condotti, had got to the first barricade, when*

*Gradually, thinking still of St. Peter's, I became conscious*

*Of a sensation of movement opposing me,—tendency this way*

*(Such as one fancies may be in a stream when the wave of the tide is*

*Coming and not yet come,—a sort of noise and retention);*

*So I turned, and, before I turned, caught sight of stragglers*

*Heading a crowd, it is plain, that is coming behind that corner.*

*Looking up, I see windows filled with heads; the Piazza,*

*Into which you remember the Ponte St. Angelo enters,*

*Since I passed, has thickened with curious groups; and now the*

*Crowd is coming, has turned, has crossed that last barricade, is*

*Here at my side. In the middle they drag at something. What is it?*

*Ha! bare swords in the air, held up? There seem to be voices*

*Pleading and hands putting back; official, perhaps; but the swords are*

*Many, and bare in the air. In the air? they descend; they are smiting,*

*Hewing, chopping—At what? In the air once more upstretched? And—*

*Is it blood that's on them? Yes, certainly blood! Of whom, then?*
*Over whom is the cry of this furor of exultation?*

  *While they are skipping and screaming, and dancing their caps on the points of*
*Swords and bayonets, I to the outskirts back, and ask a*
*Mercantile-seeming bystander, 'What is it?' and he, looking always*
*That way, makes me answer, 'A Priest, who was trying to fly to*
*The Neapolitan army,'—and thus explains the proceeding.*

  *You didn't see the dead man? No;—I began to be doubtful;*
*I was in black myself, and didn't know what mightn't happen,—*
*But a National Guard close by me, outside of the hubbub,*
*Broke his sword with slashing a broad hat covered with dust,—and*
*Passing away from the place with Murray under my arm, and*
*Stooping, I saw through the legs of the people the legs of a body.*

  *You are the first, do you know, to whom I have mentioned the matter.*
*Whom should I tell it to else?—these girls?—the Heavens forbid it!—*
*Quidnuncs at Monaldini's—Idlers upon the Pincian?*

  *If I rightly remember, it happened on that afternoon when*
*Word of the nearer approach of a new Neapolitan army*
*First was spread. I began to bethink me of Paris Septembers,*
*Thought I could fancy the look of that old 'Ninety-two. On that evening*
*Three or four, or, it may be, five, of these people were slaughtered*
*Some declared they had, one of them, fired on a sentinel; others*
*Say they were only escaping; a Priest, it is currently stated,*
*Stabbed a National Guard on the very Piazza Colonna:*
*History, Rumour of Rumours, I leave to thee to determine!*

  *But I am thankful to say the government seems to have strength to*
*Put it down; it has vanished, at least; the place is most peaceful.*
*Through the Trastevere walking last night, at nine of the clock, I*
*Found no sort of disorder; I crossed by the Island-bridges,*

*So by the narrow streets to the Ponte Rotto, and onwards*
*Thence by the Temple of Vesta, away to the great Coliseum,*
*Which at the full of the moon is an object worthy a visit.*
*VIII. Georgina Trevellyn to Louisa ——.*


*Only think, dearest Louisa, what fearful scenes we have witnessed!—*
    *      *      *      *      *      *      *      **

*George has just seen Garibaldi, dressed up in a long white cloak, on*
*Horseback, riding by, with his mounted negro behind him:*
*This is a man, you know, who came from America with him,*
*Out of the woods, I suppose, and uses a lasso in fighting,*
*Which is, I don't quite know, but a sort of noose, I imagine;*
*This he throws on the heads of the enemy's men in a battle,*
*Pulls them into his reach, and then most cruelly kills them:*
*Mary does not believe, but we heard it from an Italian.*
*Mary allows she was wrong about Mr. Claude BEING SELFISH;*
*He was MOST useful and kind on the terrible thirtieth of April.*
*Do not write here any more; we are starting directly for Florence:*
*We should be off to-morrow, if only Papa could get horses;*
*All have been seized everywhere for the use of this dreadful Mazzini*


*P.S.*
  *Mary has seen thus far.—I am really so angry, Louisa,—*
*Quite out of patience, my dearest! What can the man be intending?*
*I am quite tired; and Mary, who might bring him to in a moment,*
*Lets him go on as he likes, and neither will help nor dismiss him.*
*IX. Claude to Eustace.*


*It is most curious to see what a power a few calm words (in*

*Merely a brief proclamation) appear to possess on the people.*
*Order is perfect, and peace; the city is utterly tranquil;*
*And one cannot conceive that this easy and nonchalant crowd, that*
*Flows like a quiet stream through street and market-place, entering*
*Shady recesses and bays of church, osteria, and caffe,*
*Could in a moment be changed to a flood as of molten lava,*
*Boil into deadly wrath and wild homicidal delusion.*
  *Ah, 'tis an excellent race,—and even in old degradation,*
*Under a rule that enforces to flattery, lying, and cheating,*
*E'en under Pope and Priest, a nice and natural people.*
*Oh, could they but be allowed this chance of redemption!—but clearly*
*That is not likely to be.  Meantime, notwithstanding all journals,*
*Honour for once to the tongue and the pen of the eloquent writer!*
*Honour to speech! and all honour to thee, thou noble Mazzini!*
*X. Claude to Eustace.*


*I am in love, meantime, you think; no doubt you would think so.*
*I am in love, you say; with those letters, of course, you would say so.*
*I am in love, you declare.  I think not so; yet I grant you*
*It is a pleasure indeed to converse with this girl.  Oh, rare gift,*
*Rare felicity, this! she can talk in a rational way, can*
*Speak upon subjects that really are matters of mind and of thinking,*
*Yet in perfection retain her simplicity; never, one moment,*
*Never, however you urge it, however you tempt her, consents to*
*Step from ideas and fancies and loving sensations to those vain*
*Conscious understandings that vex the minds of mankind.*
*No, though she talk, it is music; her fingers desert not the keys; 'tis*
*Song, though you hear in the song the articulate vocables sounded,*
*Syllabled singly and sweetly the words of melodious meaning.*

*I am in love, you say; I do not think so, exactly.*
*XI. Claude to Eustace.*


*There are two different kinds, I believe, of human attraction:*
*One which simply disturbs, unsettles, and makes you uneasy,*
*And another that poises, retains, and fixes and holds you.*
*I have no doubt, for myself, in giving my voice for the latter.*
*I do not wish to be moved, but growing where I was growing,*
*There more truly to grow, to live where as yet I had languished.*
*I do not like being moved: for the will is excited; and action*
*Is a most dangerous thing; I tremble for something factitious,*
*Some malpractice of heart and illegitimate process;*
*We are so prone to these things, with our terrible notions of duty.*
*XII. Claude to Eustace.*


*Ah, let me look, let me watch, let me wait, unhurried, unprompted!*
*Bid me not venture on aught that could alter or end what is present!*
*Say not, Time flies, and Occasion, that never returns, is departing!*
*Drive me not out yet, ye ill angels with fiery swords, from my Eden,*
*Waiting, and watching, and looking! Let love be its own inspiration!*
*Shall not a voice, if a voice there must be, from the airs that environ,*
*Yea, from the conscious heavens, without our knowledge or effort,*
*Break into audible words? And love be its own inspiration?*
*XIII. Claude to Eustace.*


*Wherefore and how I am certain, I hardly can tell; but it IS so.*
*She doesn't like me, Eustace; I think she never will like me.*
*Is it my fault, as it is my misfortune, my ways are not her ways?*
*Is it my fault, that my habits and modes are dissimilar wholly?*

'Tis not her fault; 'tis her nature, her virtue, to misapprehend them:
'Tis not her fault; 'tis her beautiful nature, not ever to know me.
Hopeless it seems,—yet I cannot, though hopeless, determine to leave it:
She goes—therefore I go; she moves,—I move, not to lose her.
XIV. Claude to Eustace.


Oh, 'tisn't manly, of course, 'tisn't manly, this method of wooing;
'Tisn't the way very likely to win. For the woman, they tell you,
Ever prefers the audacious, the wilful, the vehement hero;
She has no heart for the timid, the sensitive soul; and for knowledge,—
Knowledge, O ye Gods!—when did they appreciate knowledge?
Wherefore should they, either? I am sure I do not desire it.
  Ah, and I feel too, Eustace, she cares not a tittle about me!
(Care about me, indeed! and do I really expect it?)
But my manner offends; my ways are wholly repugnant;
Every word that I utter estranges, hurts, and repels her;
Every moment of bliss that I gain, in her exquisite presence,
Slowly, surely, withdraws her, removes her, and severs her from me.
Not that I care very much!—any way I escape from the boy's own
Folly, to which I am prone, of loving where it is easy.
Not that I mind very much! Why should I? I am not in love, and
Am prepared, I think, if not by previous habit,
Yet in the spirit beforehand for this and all that is like it;
It is an easier matter for us contemplative creatures,
Us upon whom the pressure of action is laid so lightly;
We, discontented indeed with things in particular, idle,
Sickly, complaining, by faith, in the vision of things in general,
Manage to hold on our way without, like others around us,
Seizing the nearest arm to comfort, help, and support us.

*Yet, after all, my Eustace, I know but little about it.*
*All I can say for myself, for present alike and for past, is,*
*Mary Trevellyn, Eustace, is certainly worth your acquaintance.*
*You couldn't come, I suppose, as far as Florence to see her?*
*XV. Georgina Trevellyn to Louisa* ——.


*...... To-morrow we're starting for Florence,*
*Truly rejoiced, you may guess, to escape from republican terrors;*
*Mr. C. and Papa to escort us; we by vettura*
*Through Siena, and Georgy to follow and join us by Leghorn.*
*Then—— Ah, what shall I say, my dearest? I tremble in thinking!*
*You will imagine my feelings,—the blending of hope and of sorrow.*
*How can I bear to abandon Papa and Mamma and my Sisters?*
*Dearest Louise, indeed it is very alarming; but, trust me*
*Ever, whatever may change, to remain your loving Georgina.*


*P.S. by Mary Trevellyn.*


*....... 'Do I like Mr. Claude any better?'*
*I am to tell you,—and, 'Pray, is it Susan or I that attract him?'*
*This he never has told, but Georgina could certainly ask him.*
*All I can say for myself is, alas! that he rather repels me.*
*There! I think him agreeable, but also a little repulsive.*
*So be content, dear Louisa; for one satisfactory marriage*
*Surely will do in one year for the family you would establish*
*Neither Susan nor I shall afford you the joy of a second.*


*P.S. by Georgina Trevellyn.*

*Mr. Claude, you must know, is behaving a little bit better;*
*He and Papa are great friends; but he really is too SHILLY-SHALLY,—*
*So unlike George! Yet I hope that the matte is going on fairly.*
*I shall, however, get George, before he goes, to say something.*
*Dearest Louise, how delightful to bring young people together!*

---

*Is it Florence we follow, or are we to tarry yet longer,*
*E'en amid clamour of arms, here in the city of old,*
*Seeking from clamour of arms in the Past and the Arts to be hidden,*
*Vainly 'mid Arts and the Past seeking one life to forget?*
*Ah, fair shadow, scarce seen, go forth! for anon he shall follow,—*
*He that beheld thee, anon, whither thou leadest must go!*
*Go, and the wise, loving Muse, she also will follow and find thee!*
*She, should she linger in Rome, were not dissevered from thee!*

# Canto III

*Yet to the wondrous St. Peter's, and yet to the solemn Rotunda,*
  *Mingling with heroes and gods, yet to the Vatican Walls,*
*Yet may we go, and recline, while a whole mighty world seems above us,*
  *Gathered and fixed to all time into one roofing supreme;*
*Yet may we, thinking on these things, exclude what is meaner around us;*
  *Yet, at the worst of the worst, books and a chamber remain;*
*Yet may we think, and forget, and possess our souls in resistance.—*
  *Ah, but away from the stir, shouting, and gossip of war,*
*Where, upon Apennine slope, with the chestnut the oak-trees immingle,*
  *Where, amid odorous copse bridle-paths wander and wind,*
*Where, under mulberry-branches, the diligent rivulet sparkles,*
  *Or amid cotton and maize peasants their water-works ply,*
*Where, over fig-tree and orange in tier upon tier still repeated,*
  *Garden on garden upreared, balconies step to the sky,—*
*Ah, that I were far away from the crowd and the streets of the city,*
  *Under the vine-trellis laid, O my beloved, with thee!*
*I. Mary Trevellyn to Miss Roper,—on the way to Florence.*


*Why doesn't Mr. Claude come with us? you ask.—We don't know,*
*You should know better than we. He talked of the Vatican marbles;*
*But I can't wholly believe that this was the actual reason,—*
*He was so ready before, when we asked him to come and escort us.*
*Certainly he is odd, my dear Miss Roper. To change so*
*Suddenly, just for a whim, was not quite fair to the party,—*
*Not quite right. I declare, I really almost am offended:*
*I, his great friend, as you say, have doubtless a title to be so.*

*Not that I greatly regret it, for dear Georgina distinctly*
*Wishes for nothing so much as to show her adroitness.  But, oh, my*
*Pen will not write any more;—let us say nothing further about it.*
    \*   \*   \*   \*   \*   \*   \*   \*

*Yes, my dear Miss Roper, I certainly called him repulsive;*
*So I think him, but cannot be sure I have used the expression*
*Quite as your pupil should; yet he does most truly repel me.*
*Was it to you I made use of the word? or who was it told you?*
*Yes, repulsive; observe, it is but when he talks of ideas*
*That he is quite unaffected, and free, and expansive, and easy;*
*I could pronounce him simply a cold intellectual being.—*
*When does he make advances?—He thinks that women should woo him;*
*Yet, if a girl should do so, would be but alarmed and disgusted.*
*She that should love him must look for small love in return,—like the ivy*
*On the stone wall, must expect but a rigid and niggard support, and*
*E'en to get that must go searching all round with her humble embraces.*
*II. Claude to Eustace,—from Rome.*

*Tell me, my friend, do you think that the grain would sprout in the furrow,*
*Did it not truly accept as its summum and ultimum bonum*
*That mere common and may-be indifferent soil it is set in?*
*Would it have force to develop and open its young cotyledons,*
*Could it compare, and reflect, and examine one thing with another?*
*Would it endure to accomplish the round of its natural functions*
*Were it endowed with a sense of the general scheme of existence?*
  *While from Marseilles in the steamer we voyage to Civita Vecchia,*
*Vexed in the squally seas as we lay by Capraja and Elba,*
*Standing, uplifted, alone on the heaving poop of the vessel,*
*Looking around on the waste of the rushing incurious billows,*

*'This is Nature,' I said: 'we are born as it were from her waters;*
*Over her billows that buffet and beat us, her offspring uncared-for,*
*Casting one single regard of a painful victorious knowledge,*
*Into her billows that buffet and beat us we sink and are swallowed.'*
*This was the sense in my soul, as I swayed with the poop of the steamer;*
*And as unthinking I sat in the hall of the famed Ariadne,*
*Lo, it looked at me there from the face of a Triton in marble.*
*It is the simpler thought, and I can believe it the truer.*
*Let us not talk of growth; we are still in our Aqueous Ages.*
*III. Claude to Eustace.*


*Farewell, Politics, utterly! What can I do? I cannot*
*Fight, you know; and to talk I am wholly ashamed. And although I*
*Gnash my teeth when I look in your French or your English papers,*
*What is the good of that? Will swearing, I wonder, mend matters?*
*Cursing and scolding repel the assailants? No, it is idle;*
*No, whatever befalls, I will hide, will ignore or forget it.*
*Let the tail shift for itself; I will bury my head. And what's the*
*Roman Republic to me, or I to the Roman Republic?*
*Why not fight?—In the first place, I haven't so much as a musket;*
*In the next, if I had, I shouldn't know how I should use it;*
*In the third, just at present I'm studying ancient marbles;*
*In the fourth, I consider I owe my life to my country;*
*In the fifth—I forget, but four good reasons are ample.*
*Meantime, pray let 'em fight, and be killed. I delight in devotion.*
*So that I 'list not, hurrah for the glorious army of martyrs!*
*Sanguis martyrum semen Ecclesiae; though it would seem this*
*Church is indeed of the purely Invisible, Kingdom-come kind:*
*Militant here on earth! Triumphant, of course, then, elsewhere!*

*Ah, good Heaven, but I would I were out far away from the pother!*
*IV. Claude to Eustace.*


*Not, as we read in the words of the olden-time inspiration,*
*Are there two several trees in the place we are set to abide in;*
*But on the apex most high of the Tree of Life in the Garden,*
*Budding, unfolding, and falling, decaying and flowering ever,*
*Flowering is set and decaying the transient blossom of Knowledge,—*
*Flowering alone, and decaying, the needless unfruitful blossom.*
  *Or as the cypress-spires by the fair-flowing stream Hellespontine,*
*Which from the mythical tomb of the godlike Protesilaus*
*Rose sympathetic in grief to his love-lorn Laodamia,*
*Evermore growing, and when in their growth to the prospect attaining,*
*Over the low sea-banks, of the fatal Ilian city,*
*Withering still at the sight which still they upgrow to encounter.*
  *Ah, but ye that extrude from the ocean your helpless faces,*
*Ye over stormy seas leading long and dreary processions,*
*Ye, too, brood of the wind, whose coming is whence we discern not,*
*Making your nest on the wave, and your bed on the crested billow,*
*Skimming rough waters, and crowding wet sands that the tide shall return to,*
*Cormorants, ducks, and gulls, fill ye my imagination!*
*Let us not talk of growth; we are still in our Aqueous Ages.*
*V. Mary Trevellyn to Miss Roper,—from Florence.*


*Dearest Miss Roper,—Alas! we are all at Florence quite safe, and*
*You, we hear, are shut up! indeed, it is sadly distressing!*
*We were most lucky, they say, to get off when we did from the troubles.*
*Now you are really besieged; they tell us it soon will be over;*
*Only I hope and trust without any fight in the city.*

*Do you see Mr. Claude?—I thought he might do something for you.*

*I am quite sure on occasion he really would wish to be useful.*

*What is he doing? I wonder;—still studying Vatican marbles?*

*Letters, I hope, pass through. We trust your brother is better.*

*VI. Claude to Eustace.*


*Juxtaposition, in fine; and what is juxtaposition?*

*Look you, we travel along in the railway-carriage or steamer,*

*And, pour passer le temps, till the tedious journey be ended,*

*Lay aside paper or book, to talk with the girl that is next one;*

*And, pour passer le temps, with the terminus all but in prospect,*

*Talk of eternal ties and marriages made in heaven.*

*Ah, did we really accept with a perfect heart the illusion!*

*Ah, did we really believe that the Present indeed is the Only!*

*Or through all transmutation, all shock and convulsion of passion,*

*Feel we could carry undimmed, unextinguished, the light of our knowledge!*

*But for his funeral train which the bridegroom sees in the distance,*

*Would he so joyfully, think you, fall in with the marriage procession?*

*But for that final discharge, would he dare to enlist in that service?*

*But for that certain release, ever sign to that perilous contract?*

*But for that exit secure, ever bend to that treacherous doorway?—*

*Ah, but the bride, meantime,—do you think she sees it as he does?*

*But for the steady fore-sense of a freer and larger existence,*

*Think you that man could consent to be circumscribed here into action?*

*But for assurance within a limitless ocean divine, o'er*

*Whose great tranquil depths unconscious the wind-tost surface*

*Breaks into ripples of trouble that come and change and endure not,—*

*But that in this, of a truth, we have our being, and know it,*

*Think you we men could submit to live and move as we do here?*

*Ah, but the women,—God bless them! they don't think at all about it.*

*Yet we must eat and drink, as you say.  And as limited beings*
*Scarcely can hope to attain upon earth to an Actual Abstract,*
*Leaving to God contemplation, to His hands knowledge confiding,*
*Sure that in us if it perish, in Him it abideth and dies not,*
*Let us in His sight accomplish our petty particular doings,—*
*Yes, and contented sit down to the victual that He has provided.*
*Allah is great, no doubt, and Juxtaposition his prophet.*
*Ah, but the women, alas! they don't look at it that way.*
*Juxtaposition is great;—but, my friend, I fear me, the maiden*
*Hardly would thank or acknowledge the lover that sought to obtain her,*
*Not as the thing he would wish, but the thing he must even put up with,—*
*Hardly would tender her hand to the wooer that candidly told her*
*That she is but for a space, an ad-interim solace and pleasure,—*
*That in the end she shall yield to a perfect and absolute something,*
*Which I then for myself shall behold, and not another,—*
*Which amid fondest endearments, meantime I forget not, forsake not*
*Ah, ye feminine souls, so loving, and so exacting,*
*Since we cannot escape, must we even submit to deceive you?*
*Since, so cruel is truth, sincerity shocks and revolts you,*
*Will you have us your slaves to lie to you, flatter and—leave you?*
*VII. Claude to Eustace.*


*Juxtaposition is great,—but, you tell me, affinity greater.*
*Ah, my friend, there are many affinities, greater and lesser,*
*Stronger and weaker; and each, by the favour of juxtaposition,*
*Potent, efficient, in force,—for a time; but none, let me tell you,*
*Save by the law of the land and the ruinous force of the will, ah,*
*None, I fear me, at last quite sure to be final and perfect.*

*Lo, as I pace in the street, from the peasant-girl to the princess,*
*Homo sum, nihil humani a me alienum puto,—*
*Vir sum, nihil faeminei,—and e'en to the uttermost circle,*
*All that is Nature's is I, and I all things that are Nature's.*
*Yes, as I walk, I behold, in a luminous, large intuition,*
*That I can be and become anything that I meet with or look at:*
*I am the ox in the dray, the ass with the garden-stuff panniers;*
*I am the dog in the doorway, the kitten that plays in the window,*
*On sunny slab of the ruin the furtive and fugitive lizard,*
*Swallow above me that twitters, and fly that is buzzing about me;*
*Yea, and detect, as I go, by a faint but a faithful assurance,*
*E'en from the stones of the street, as from rocks or trees of the forest,*
*Something of kindred, a common, though latent vitality, greets me;*
*And to escape from our strivings, mistakings, misgrowths, and perversions,*
*Fain could demand to return to that perfect and primitive silence,*
*Fain be enfolded and fixed, as of old, in their rigid embraces.*
*VIII. Claude to Eustace.*

*And as I walk on my way, I behold them consorting and coupling;*
*Faithful it seemeth, and fond, very fond, very probably faithful,*
*All as I go on my way, with a pleasure sincere and unmingled.*
  *Life is beautiful, Eustace, entrancing, enchanting to look at;*
*As are the streets of a city we pace while the carriage is changing,*
*As a chamber filled-in with harmonious, exquisite pictures,*
*Even so beautiful Earth; and could we eliminate only*
*This vile hungering impulse, this demon within us of craving,*
*Life were beatitude, living a perfect divine satisfaction.*
*IX. Claude to Eustace.*

*Mild monastic faces in quiet collegiate cloisters:*
*So let me offer a single and celibatarian phrase, a*
*Tribute to those whom perhaps you do not believe I can honour.*
*But, from the tumult escaping, 'tis pleasant, of drumming and shouting,*
*Hither, oblivious awhile, to withdraw, of the fact or the falsehood,*
*And amid placid regards and mildly courteous greetings*
*Yield to the calm and composure and gentle abstraction that reign o'er*
*Mild monastic faces in quiet collegiate cloisters.*

*Terrible word, Obligation! You should not, Eustace, you should not,*
*No, you should not have used it. But, oh, great Heavens, I repel it!*
*Oh, I cancel, reject, disavow, and repudiate wholly*
*Every debt in this kind, disclaim every claim, and dishonour,*
*Yea, my own heart's own writing, my soul's own signature! Ah, no!*
*I will be free in this; you shall not, none shall, bind me.*
*No, my friend, if you wish to be told, it was this above all things,*
*This that charmed me, ah, yes, even this, that she held me to nothing.*
*No, I could talk as I pleased; come close; fasten ties, as I fancied;*
*Bind and engage myself deep;—and lo, on the following morning*
*It was all e'en as before, like losings in games played for nothing.*
*Yes, when I came, with mean fears in my soul, with a semi-performance*
*At the first step breaking down in its pitiful role of evasion,*
*When to shuffle I came, to compromise, not meet, engagements,*
*Lo, with her calm eyes there she met me and knew nothing of it,—*
*Stood unexpecting, unconscious. SHE spoke not of obligations,*
*Knew not of debt—ah, no, I believe you, for excellent reasons.*
*X. Claude to Eustace.*

*HANG this thinking, at last! what good is it? oh, and what evil!*
*Oh, what mischief and pain! like a clock in a sick man's chamber,*

*Ticking and ticking, and still through each covert of slumber pursuing.*

  *What shall I do to thee, O thou Preserver of men? Have compassion;*

*Be favourable, and hear! Take from me this regal knowledge;*

*Let me, contented and mute, with the beasts of the fields, my brothers,*

*Tranquilly, happily lie,—and eat grass, like Nebuchadnezzar!*

*XI. Claude to Eustace.*


*Tibur is beautiful, too, and the orchard slopes, and the Anio*

*Falling, falling yet, to the ancient lyrical cadence;*

*Tibur and Anio's tide; and cool from Lucretilis ever,*

*With the Digentian stream, and with the Bandusian fountain,*

*Folded in Sabine recesses, the valley and villa of Horace:—*

*So not seeing I sang; so seeing and listening say I,*

*Here as I sit by the stream, as I gaze at the cell of the Sibyl,*

*Here with Albunea's home and the grove of Tiburnus beside me; [\*]*

*Tivoli beautiful is, and musical, O Teverone,*

*Dashing from mountain to plain, thy parted impetuous waters,*

*Tivoli's waters and rocks; and fair unto Monte Gennaro*

*(Haunt, even yet, I must think, as I wander and gaze, of the shadows,*

*Faded and pale, yet immortal, of Faunus, the Nymphs, and the Graces).*

*Fair in itself, and yet fairer with human completing creations,*

*Folded in Sabine recesses the valley and villa of Horace:—*

*So not seeing I sang; so now—Nor seeing, nor hearing,*

*Neither by waterfall lulled, nor folded in sylvan embraces,*

*Neither by cell of the Sibyl, nor stepping the Monte Gennaro,*

*Seated on Anio's bank, nor sipping Bandusian waters,*

*But on Montorio's height, looking down on the tile-clad streets, the*

*Cupolas, crosses, and domes, the bushes and kitchen-gardens,*

*Which, by the grace of the Tibur, proclaim themselves Rome of the Romans,—*

*But on Montorio's height, looking forth to the vapoury mountains,*
*Cheating the prisoner Hope with illusions of vision and fancy,—*
*But on Montorio's height, with these weary soldiers by me,*
*Waiting till Oudinot enter, to reinstate Pope and Tourist.*


    *  — domus Albuneae resonantis,*
      *Et praeceps Anio, et Tibuni lucus, et uda*
        *Mobilibus pomaria rivis*
*XII. Mary Trevellyn to Miss Roper.*


*Dear Miss Roper,—It seems, George Vernon, before we left Rome, said*
*Something to Mr. Claude about what they call his attentions.*
*Susan, two nights ago, for the first time, heard this from Georgina.*
*It is SO disagreeable and SO annoying to think of!*
*If it could only be known, though we may never meet him again, that*
*It was all George's doing, and we were entirely unconscious,*
*It would extremely relieve—Your ever affectionate Mary.*


*P.S. (1)*

  *Here is your letter arrived this moment, just as I wanted.*
*So you have seen him,—indeed, and guessed,—how dreadfully clever!*
*What did he really say? and what was your answer exactly?*
*Charming!—but wait for a moment, I haven't read through the letter.*


*P.S. (2)*

  *Ah, my dearest Miss Roper, do just as you fancy about it.*
*If you think it sincerer to tell him I know of it, do so.*
*Though I should most extremely dislike it, I know I could manage.*
*It is the simplest thing, but surely wholly uncalled for.*

*Do as you please; you know I trust implicitly to you.*
*Say whatever is right and needful for ending the matter.*
*Only don't tell Mr. Claude, what I will tell you as a secret,*
*That I should like very well to show him myself I forget it.*

*P.S. (3)*

*I am to say that the wedding is finally settled for Tuesday.*
*Ah, my dear Miss Roper, you surely, surely can manage*
*Not to let it appear that I know of that odious matter.*
*It would be pleasanter far for myself to treat it exactly*
*As if it had not occurred: and I do not think he would like it.*
*I must remember to add, that as soon as the wedding is over*
*We shall be off, I believe, in a hurry, and travel to Milan;*
*There to meet friends of Papa's, I am told, at the Croce di Malta*
*Then I cannot say whither, but not at present to England.*
*XIII. Claude to Eustace.*

*Yes, on Montorio's height for a last farewell of the city,—*
*So it appears; though then I was quite uncertain about it.*
*So, however, it was. And now to explain the proceeding.*
*I was to go, as I told you, I think, with the people to Florence.*
*Only the day before, the foolish family Vernon*
*Made some uneasy remarks, as we walked to our lodging together,*
*As to intentions forsooth, and so forth. I was astounded,*
*Horrified quite; and obtaining just then, as it happened, an offer*
*(No common favour) of seeing the great Ludovisi collection,*
*Why, I made this a pretence, and wrote that they must excuse me.*
*How could I go? Great Heavens! to conduct a permitted flirtation*
*Under those vulgar eyes, the observed of such observers!*

*Well, but I now, by a series of fine diplomatic inquiries,*

*Find from a sort of relation, a good and sensible woman,*

*Who is remaining at Rome with a brother too ill for removal,*

*That it was wholly unsanctioned, unknown,—not, I think, by Georgina:*

*She, however, ere this,—and that is the best of the story,—*

*She and the Vernon, thank Heaven, are wedded and gone—honey-mooning.*

*So—on Montorio's height for a last farewell of the city.*

*Tibur I have not seen, nor the lakes that of old I had dreamt of;*

*Tibur I shall not see, nor Anio's waters, nor deep en-*

*Folded in Sabine recesses the valley and villa of Horace;*

*Tibur I shall not see;—but something better I shall see.*

  *Twice I have tried before, and failed in getting the horses;*

*Twice I have tried and failed: this time it shall not be a failure.*

*Therefore farewell, ye hills, and ye, ye envineyarded ruins!*

  *Therefore farewell, ye walls, palaces, pillars, and domes!*

*Therefore farewell, far seen, ye peaks of the mythic Albano,*

  *Seen from Montorio's height, Tibur and Aesula's hills!*

*Ah, could we once, ere we go, could we stand, while, to ocean descending,*

  *Sinks o'er the yellow dark plain slowly the yellow broad sun,*

*Stand, from the forest emerging at sunset, at once in the champaign,*

  *Open, but studded with trees, chestnuts umbrageous and old,*

*E'en in those fair open fields that incurve to thy beautiful hollow,*

  *Nemi, imbedded in wood, Nemi, inurned in the hill!—*

*Therefore farewell, ye plains, and ye hills, and the City Eternal!*

  *Therefore farewell! We depart, but to behold you again!*

# Canto IV

*Eastward, or Northward, or West? I wander and ask as I wander;*
*Weary, yet eager and sure, Where shall I come to my love?*
*Whitherward hasten to seek her? Ye daughters of Italy, tell me,*
*Graceful and tender and dark, is she consorting with you?*
*Thou that out-climbest the torrent, that tendest thy goats to the summit,*
*Call to me, child of the Alp, has she been seen on the heights?*
*Italy, farewell I bid thee! for whither she leads me, I follow.*
*Farewell the vineyard! for I, where I but guess her, must go;*
*Weariness welcome, and labour, wherever it be, if at last it*
*Bring me in mountain or plain into the sight of my love.*
*I. Claude to Eustace,—from Florence.*

*Gone from Florence; indeed! and that is truly provoking;—*
*Gone to Milan, it seems; then I go also to Milan.*
*Five days now departed; but they can travel but slowly;—*
*I quicker far; and I know, as it happens, the home they will go to.—*
*Why, what else should I do? Stay here and look at the pictures,*
*Statues and churches? Alack, I am sick of the statues and pictures!—*
*No, to Bologna, Parma, Piacenza, Lodi, and Milan,*
*Off go we to-night,—and the Venus go to the Devil!*
*II. Claude to Eustace,—from Bellaggio.*

*Gone to Como, they said; and I have posted to Como.*
*There was a letter left; but the cameriere had lost it.*
*Could it have been for me? They came, however, to Como,*
*And from Como went by the boat,—perhaps to the Spluegen,—*

*Or to the Stelvio, say, and the Tyrol; also it might be*
*By Porlezza across to Lugano, and so to the Simplon*
*Possibly, or the St. Gothard,—or possibly, too, to Baveno,*
*Orta, Turin, and elsewhere.  Indeed, I am greatly bewildered.*
*III. Claude to Eustace,—from Bellaggio.*


*I have been up the Spluegen, and on the Stelvio also:*
*Neither of these can I find they have followed; in no one inn, and*
*This would be odd, have they written their names.  I have been to Porlezza;*
*There they have not been seen, and therefore not at Lugano.*
*What shall I do?  Go on through the Tyrol, Switzerland, Deutschland,*
*Seeking, an inverse Saul, a kingdom to find only asses?*
  *There is a tide, at least, in the LOVE affairs of mortals,*
*Which, when taken at flood, leads on to the happiest fortune,—*
*Leads to the marriage-morn and the orange-flowers and the altar,*
*And the long lawful line of crowned joys to crowned joys succeeding.—*
*Ah, it has ebbed with me!  Ye gods, and when it was flowing,*
*Pitiful fool that I was, to stand fiddle-faddling in that way!*
*IV. Claude to Eustace,—from Bellaggio.*


*I have returned and found their names in the book at Como.*
*Certain it is I was right, and yet I am also in error.*
*Added in feminine hand, I read, By the boat to Bellaggio.—*
*So to Bellaggio again, with the words of he writing to aid me.*
*Yet at Bellaggio I find no trace, no sort of remembrance.*
*So I am here, and wait, and know every hour will remove them.*
*V. Claude to Eustace,—from Bellaggio.*


*I have but one chance left,—and that is going to Florence.*

*But it is cruel to turn. The mountains seem to demand me,—*
*Peak and valley from far to beckon and motion me onward.*
*Somewhere amid their folds she passes whom fain I would follow;*
*Somewhere amid those heights she haply calls me to seek her.*
*Ah, could I hear her call! could I catch the glimpse of her raiment!*
*Turn, however, I must, though it seem I turn to desert her;*
*For the sense of the thing is simply to hurry to Florence,*
*Where the certainty yet may be learnt, I suppose, from the Ropers.*
*VI. Mary Trevellyn, from Lucerne, to Miss Roper, at Florence.*


*Dear Miss Roper,—By this you are safely away, we are hoping,*
*Many a league from Rome; ere long we trust we shall see you.*
*How have you travelled? I wonder;—was Mr. Claude your companion?*
*As for ourselves, we went from Como straight to Lugano;*
*So by the Mount St. Gothard; we meant to go by Porlezza,*
*Taking the steamer, and stopping, as you had advised, at Bellaggio,*
*Two or three days or more; but this was suddenly altered,*
*After we left the hotel, on the very way to the steamer.*
*So we have seen, I fear, not one of the lakes in perfection.*
  *Well, he is not come, and now, I suppose, he will not come.*
*What will you think, meantime? and yet I must really confess it;—*
*What will you say? I wrote him a note. We left in a hurry,*
*Went from Milan to Como, three days before we expected.*
*But I thought, if he came all the way to Milan, he really*
*Ought not to be disappointed: and so I wrote three lines to*
*Say I had heard he was coming, desirous of joining our party;—*
*If so, then I said, we had started for Como, and meant to*
*Cross the St. Gothard, and stay, we believed, at Lucerne, for the summer.*
*Was it wrong? and why, if it was, has it failed to bring him?*

*Did he not think it worth while to come to Milan? He knew (you*

*Told him) the house we should go to.  Or may it, perhaps, have miscarried?*

*Any way, now, I repent, and am heartily vexed that I wrote it.*

*There is a home on the shore of the Alpine sea, that upswelling*

  *High up the mountain-sides spreads in the hollow between;*

*Wilderness, mountain, and snow from the land of the olive conceal it;*

  *Under Pilatus's hill low by the river it lies;*

*Italy, utter the word, and the olive and vine will allure not,——*

  *Wilderness, forest, and snow will not the passage impede;*

*Italy, unto thy cities receding, the clue to recover,*

  *Hither, recovered the clue, shall not the traveller haste?*

# Canto V

*There is a city, upbuilt on the quays of the turbulent Arno,*
  *Under Fiesole's heights,—thither are we to return?*
*There is a city that fringes the curve of the inflowing waters,*
  *Under the perilous hill fringes the beautiful bay,—*
*Parthenope, do they call thee?—the Siren, Neapolis, seated*
  *Under Vesevus's hill,—are we receding to thee?—*
*Sicily, Greece, will invite, and the Orient;—or are we turn to*
  *England, which may after all be for its children the best?*
*I. Mary Trevellyn, at Lucerne, to Miss Roper, at Florence.*


*So you are really free, and living in quiet at Florence;*
*That is delightful news; you travelled slowly and safely;*
*Mr. Claude got you out; took rooms at Florence before you;*
*Wrote from Milan to say so; had left directly for Milan,*
*Hoping to find us soon;—if he could, he would, you are certain.—*
*Dear Miss Roper, your letter has made me exceedingly happy.*
  *You are quite sure, you say, he asked you about our intentions;*
*You had not heard as yet of Lucerne, but told him of Como.—*
*Well, perhaps he will come; however, I will not expect it.*
*Though you say you are sure,—if he can, he will, you are certain.*
*O my dear, many thanks from your ever affectionate Mary.*
*II. Claude to Eustace.*


*Florence.*
*Action will furnish belief,—but will that belief be the true one?*
*This is the point, you know.  However, it doesn't much matter.*

*What one wants, I suppose, is to predetermine the action,*

*So as to make it entail, not a chance belief, but the true one.*

*Out of the question, you say; if a thing isn't wrong we may do it.*

*Ah! but this WRONG, you see—but I do not know that it matters.*

*Eustace, the Ropers are gone, and no one can tell me about them.*


### Pisa.

*Pisa, they say they think, and so I follow to Pisa,*

*Hither and thither inquiring. I weary of making inquiries.*

*I am ashamed, I declare, of asking people about it.—*

*Who are your friends? You said you had friends who would certainly know them.*


### Florence.

*But it is idle, moping, and thinking, and trying to fix her*

*Image once more and more in, to write the whole perfect inscription*

*Over and over again upon every page of remembrance.*

*I have settled to stay at Florence to wait for your answer.*

*Who are your friends? Write quickly and tell me. I wait for your answer.*

*III. Mary Trevellyn to Miss Roper.—at Lucca Baths.*


*You are at Lucca baths, you tell me, to stay for the summer;*

*Florence was quite too hot; you can't move further at present.*

*Will you not come, do you think, before the summer is over?*

*Mr. C. got you out with very considerable trouble;*

*And he was useful and kind, and seemed so happy to serve you.*

*Didn't stay with you long, but talked very openly to you;*

*Made you almost his confessor, without appearing to know it,—*

*What about?—and you say you didn't need his confessions.*

*O my dear Miss Roper, I dare not trust what you tell me!*

*Will he come, do you think? I am really so sorry for him.*
*They didn't give him my letter at Milan, I feel pretty certain.*
*You had told him Bellaggio. We didn't go to Bellaggio;*
*So he would miss our track, and perhaps never come to Lugano,*
*Where we were written in full, To Lucerne across the St. Gothard.*
*But he could write to you;—you would tell him where you were going.*
*IV. Claude to Eustace.*


*Let me, then, bear to forget her. I will not cling to her falsely:*
*Nothing factitious or forced shall impair the old happy relation.*
*I will let myself go, forget, not try to remember;*
*I will walk on my way, accept the chances that meet me,*
*Freely encounter the world, imbibe these alien airs, and*
*Never ask if new feelings and thoughts are of her or of others.*
*Is she not changing herself?—the old image would only delude me.*
*I will be bold, too, and change,—if it must be. Yet if in all things,*
*Yet if I do but aspire evermore to the Absolute only,*
*I shall be doing, I think, somehow, what she will be doing;—*
*I shall be thine, O my child, some way, though I know not in what way,*
*Let me submit to forget her; I must; I already forget her.*
*V. Claude to Eustace.*


*Utterly vain is, alas! this attempt at the Absolute,—wholly!*
*I, who believed not in her, because I would fain believe nothing,*
*Have to believe as I may, with a wilful, unmeaning acceptance.*
*I, who refused to enfasten the roots of my floating existence*
*In the rich earth, cling now to the hard, naked rock that is left me,—*
*Ah! she was worthy, Eustace,—and that, indeed, is my comfort,—*
*Worthy a nobler heart than a fool such as I could have given her.*

---

*Yes, it relieves me to write, though I do not send, and the chance that*
*Takes may destroy my fragments.  But as men pray, without asking*
*Whether One really exist to hear or do anything for them,—*
*Simply impelled by the need of the moment to turn to a Being*
*In a conception of whom there is freedom from all limitation,—*
*So in your image I turn to an ens rationis of friendship,*
*Even so write in your name I know not to whom nor in what wise.*

---

*There was a time, methought it was but lately departed,*
*When, if a thing was denied me, I felt I was bound to attempt it;*
*Choice alone should take, and choice alone should surrender.*
*There was a time, indeed, when I had not retired thus early,*
*Languidly thus, from pursuit of a purpose I once had adopted,*
*But it is all over, all that!  I have slunk from the perilous field in*
*Whose wild struggle of forces the prizes of life are contested.*
*It is over, all that!  I am a coward, and know it.*
*Courage in me could be only factitious, unnatural, useless.*

---

*Comfort has come to me here in the dreary streets of the city,*
*Comfort—how do you think?—with a barrel-organ to bring it.*
*Moping along the streets, and cursing my day as I wandered,*
*All of a sudden my ear met the sound of an English psalm-tune,*

*Comfort me it did, till indeed I was very near crying.*
*Ah, there is some great truth, partial, very likely, but needful,*
*Lodged, I am strangely sure, in the tones of the English psalm-tune.*
*Comfort it was at least; and I must take without question*
*Comfort, however it come, in the dreary streets of the city.*

---

*What with trusting myself and seeking support from within me,*
*Almost I could believe I had gained a religious assurance,*
*Formed in my own poor soul a great moral basis to rest on.*
*Ah, but indeed I see, I feel it factitious entirely;*
*I refuse, reject, and put it utterly from me;*
*I will look straight out, see things, not try to evade them;*
*Fact shall be fact for me, and the Truth the Truth as ever,*
*Flexible, changeable, vague, and multiform, and doubtful.-*
*Off, and depart to the void, thou subtle, fanatical tempter!*

---

*I shall behold thee again (is it so?) at a new visitation,*
*O ill genius thou! I shall at my life's dissolution*
*(When the pulses are weak, and the feeble light of the reason*
*Flickers, an unfed flame retiring slow from the socket),*
*Low on a sick-bed laid, hear one, as it were, at the doorway,*
*And, looking up, see thee standing by, looking emptily at me;*
*I shall entreat thee then, though now I dare to refuse thee,—*
*Pale and pitiful now, but terrible then to the dying.—*
*Well, I will see thee again, and while I can, will repel thee.*

*VI. Claude to Eustace.*


*Rome is fallen, I hear, the gallant Medici taken,*
*Noble Manara slain, and Garibaldi has lost il Moro;—*
*Rome is fallen; and fallen, or falling, heroical Venice.*
*I, meanwhile, for the loss of a single small chit of a girl, sit*
*Moping and mourning here,—for her, and myself much smaller.*
  *Whither depart the souls of the brave that die in the battle,*
*Die in the lost, lost fight, for the cause that perishes with them?*
*Are they upborne from the field on the slumberous pinions of angels*
*Unto a far-off home, where the weary rest from their labour,*
*And the deep wounds are healed, and the bitter and burning moisture*
*Wiped from the generous eyes? or do they linger, unhappy,*
*Pining, and haunting the grave of their by-gone hope and endeavour?*
  *All declamation, alas! though I talk, I care not for Rome nor*
*Italy; feebly and faintly, and but with the lips, can lament the*
*Wreck of the Lombard youth, and the victory of the oppressor.*
*Whither depart the brave?—God knows; I certainly do not.*
*VII. Mary Trevellyn to Miss Roper.*


*He has not come as yet; and now I must not expect it.*
*You have written, you say, to friends at Florence, to see him,*
*If he perhaps should return;—but that is surely unlikely.*
*Has he not written to you?—he did not know your direction.*
*Oh, how strange never once to have told him where you were going!*
*Yet if he only wrote to Florence, that would have reached you.*
*If what you say he said was true, why has he not done so?*
*Is he gone back to Rome, do you think, to his Vatican marbles?—*
*O my dear Miss Roper, forgive me! do not be angry!—*

*You have written to Florence;—your friends would certainly find him.*
*Might you not write to him?—but yet it is so little likely!*
*I shall expect nothing more.—Ever yours, your affectionate Mary.*
*VIII. Claude to Eustace.*

*I cannot stay at Florence, not even to wait for a letter.*
*Galleries only oppress me.  Remembrance of hope I had cherished*
*(Almost more than as hope, when I passed through Florence the first time)*
*Lies like a sword in my soul.  I am more a coward than ever,*
*Chicken-hearted, past thought.  The caffes and waiters distress me.*
*All is unkind, and, alas! I am ready for anyone's kindness.*
*Oh, I knew it of old, and knew it, I thought, to perfection,*
*If there is any one thing in the world to preclude all kindness*
*It is the need of it,—it is this sad, self-defeating dependence.*
*Why is this, Eustace?  Myself, were I stronger, I think I could tell you.*
*But it is odd when it comes.  So plumb I the deeps of depression,*
*Daily in deeper, and find no support, no will, no purpose.*
*All my old strengths are gone.  And yet I shall have to do something.*
*Ah, the key of our life, that passes all wards, opens all locks,*
*Is not I WILL, but I MUST.  I must,—I must,—and I do it.*

---

*After all, do I know that I really cared so about her?*
*Do whatever I will, I cannot call up her image;*
*For when I close my eyes, I see, very likely, St. Peter's,*
*Or the Pantheon facade, or Michel Angelo's figures,*
*Or, at a wish, when I please, the Alban hills and the Forum,—*
*But that face, those eyes,—ah, no, never anything like them;*

*Only, try as I will, a sort of featureless outline,*
*And a pale blank orb, which no recollection will add to.*
*After all, perhaps there was something factitious about it;*
*I have had pain, it is true: I have wept; and so have the actors.*

---

*At the last moment I have your letter, for which I was waiting;*
*I have taken my place, and see no good in inquiries.*
*Do nothing more, good Eustace, I pray you. It only will vex me.*
*Take no measures. Indeed, should we meet, I could not be certain;*
*All might be changed, you know. Or perhaps there was nothing to be changed.*
*It is a curious history, this; and yet I foresaw it;*
*I could have told it before. The Fates, it is clear, are against us;*
*For it is certain enough I met with the people you mention;*
*They were at Florence the day I returned there, and spoke to me even;*
*Stayed a week, saw me often; departed, and whither I know not.*
*Great is Fate, and is best. I believe in Providence partly.*
*What is ordained is right, and all that happens is ordered.*
*Ah, no, that isn't it. But yet I retain my conclusion.*
*I will go where I am led, and will not dictate to the chances.*
*Do nothing more, I beg. If you love me, forbear interfering.*
*IX. Claude to Eustace.*

*Shall we come out of it all, some day, as one does from a tunnel?*
*Will it be all at once, without our doing or asking,*
*We shall behold clear day, the trees and meadows about us,*
*And the faces of friends, and the eyes we loved looking at us?*
*Who knows? Who can say? It will not do to suppose it.*

*X. Claude to Eustace,-from Rome.*

*Rome will not suit me, Eustace; the priests and soldiers possess it;*
*Priests and soldiers:—and, ah! which is the worst, the priest or the soldier?*
*Politics, farewell, however! For what could I do? with inquiring,*
*Talking, collating the journals, go fever my brain about things o'er*
*Which I can have no control. No, happen whatever may happen,*
*Time, I suppose, will subsist; the earth will revolve on its axis;*
*People will travel; the stranger will wander as now in the city;*
*Rome will be here, and the Pope the custode of Vatican marbles.*
*I have no heart, however, for any marble or fresco;*
*I have essayed it in vain; 'tis in vain as yet to essay it:*
*But I may haply resume some day my studies in this kind;*
*Not as the Scripture says, is, I think, the fact. Ere our death-day,*
*Faith, I think, does pass, and Love; but Knowledge abideth.*
*Let us seek Knowledge;—the rest may come and go as it happens.*
*Knowledge is hard to seek, and harder yet to adhere to.*
*Knowledge is painful often; and yet when we know we are happy.*
*Seek it, and leave mere Faith and Love to come with the chances.*
*As for Hope,—to-morrow I hope to be starting for Naples.*
*Rome will not do, I see, for many very good reasons.*
*Eastward, then, I suppose, with the coming of winter, to Egypt.*
*XI. Mary Trevellyn to Miss Roper.*

*You have heard nothing; of course I know you can have heard nothing.*
*Ah, well, more than once I have broken my purpose, and sometimes,*
*Only too often, have looked for the little lake steamer to bring him.*
*But it is only fancy,—I do not really expect it.*
*Oh, and you see I know so exactly how he would take it:*

*Finding the chances prevail against meeting again, he would banish*
*Forthwith every thought of the poor little possible hope, which*
*I myself could not help, perhaps, thinking only too much of;*
*He would resign himself, and go.  I see it exactly.*
*So I also submit, although in a different manner.*
   *Can you not really come?  We go very shortly to England.*

---

*So go forth to the world, to the good report and the evil!*
   *Go, little book! thy tale, is it not evil and good?*
*Go, and if strangers revile, pass quietly by without answer.*
   *Go, and if curious friends ask of thy rearing and age,*
*Say, 'I am flitting about many years from brain unto brain of*
   *Feeble and restless youths born to inglorious days:*
*But,' so finish the word, 'I was writ in a Roman chamber,*
   *When from Janiculan heights thundered the cannon of France.'*

Printed by BoD™in Norderstedt, Germany